friend me

DISCUSSION GUIDE

Donna Carter

WHITAKER
HOUSE

Unless otherwise indicated, all Scripture quotations are taken from the *Holy Bible, New Living Translation*, © 1996. Used by permission of Tyndale House Publishers, Inc., Carol Stream, Illinois 60188. All rights reserved. Scripture quotations marked (MSG) are taken from *The Message: The Bible in Contemporary Language* by Eugene H. Peterson, © 1993, 1994, 1995, 1996, 2000, 2001, 2002. Used by permission of NavPress Publishing Group. All rights reserved. Scripture quotations marked (TLB) are taken from *The Living Bible*, © 1971. Used by permission of Tyndale House Publishers, Inc., Wheaton, Illinois 60189. All rights reserved. Scripture quotations marked (NIV) are taken from the *Holy Bible, New International Version*®, NIV®, © 1973, 1978, 1984 by the International Bible Society. Used by permission of Zondervan. All rights reserved. Scripture quotation marked (KJV) is taken from the King James Version of the Holy Bible. Scripture quotation marked (NLT07) is taken from the *Holy Bible, New Living Translation*, © 1996, 2004, 2007. Used by permission of Tyndale House Publishers, Inc., Carol Stream, Illinois 60188. All rights reserved.

FRIEND ME DISCUSSION GUIDE
A companion to *Friend Me: Turning Faces into Lasting Friendships*
& the accompanying DVD

Straight Talk Ministries
donnacarter.org ♦ 1.866.835.5827

The author is represented by
MacGregor Literary, Inc., of Hillsboro, Oregon.

ISBN: 978-1-60374-804-9
Printed in the United States of America
© 2013 by Donna Carter

Whitaker House
1030 Hunt Valley Circle
New Kensington, PA 15068
www.whitakerhouse.com

No part of this book may be reproduced or transmitted in any form or by any means, electronic or mechanical—including photocopying, recording, or by any information storage and retrieval system—without permission in writing from the publisher. Please direct your inquiries to permissionseditor@whitakerhouse.com.

CONTENTS

A Note to the Participant..4

Part I: The Power of Friendship
1. Just One Friend..5
2. Everyone Needs a Friend...7

Part II: The Portrait of Friendship
3. Being There..13
4. The Blonde Leading the Blonde......................................19
5. A Soft Place to Fall..25

Part III: The Path of Friendship
6. How to Build a Friendship...32
7. Toxic Friendships..37
8. Mending Fences..46

Part IV: The Privilege of Friendship
9. When You Can't Find a Friend......................................54
10. The Perfect Friend..60

Conclusion..65
Read Before You Lead...69
About the Author..75

A NOTE TO THE PARTICIPANT

Welcome to the *Friend Me* experience, where we will explore real relationships with real people in real time. This participant's guide is designed to help you interact with the material presented in the book and on the DVD during a time of discussion with the other members of your small group.

Every chapter of this guide features several distinct sections to enhance your experience. The first section is entitled "Watch It." Here, you may take notes or jot down any questions that come to mind while you watch the DVD, so that you may discuss them later on with your small group. This section also contains many of the key points and Scriptures from the teaching segments. The next section, "Talk It," includes questions to guide your personal reflections and/or conversation with your small group. Finally, the section entitled "Walk It" is intended to help you apply what you have learned to your day-to-day life of relationships.

My hope is that as you learn about turning faces into lasting friendships, you will gain fresh insights in understanding yourself and enter into new levels of maturity and fulfillment in your relationships with others and with God.

—*Donna Carter*

1

JUST ONE FRIEND

Watch It

As you watch today's DVD session or as you read chapter one, lean into this powerful story of friendship with an open heart.

Talk It

1. Who were your closest friends in childhood and throughout adolescence? What was the basis for these friendships? (In other words, what common ground did you share?)

2. Were any of your childhood friendships similar to Donna's deep friendship with Sonja? How so? How were they different?

3. What role did your earliest friendships play in establishing the foundation for future relationships in your life?

4. If you had the opportunity to express your appreciation to your closest childhood friend, what would you say?

5. What's stopping you?

Walk It

Whom will you affirm this week for his or her positive presence in your life?

2

EVERYONE NEEDS A FRIEND

Watch It

Many women are lonely and desperate for community with other women. Their question is: "How can I find a true friend?"

Some stumbling blocks to satisfying friendship:
- Fear of being truly known
- Fear of rejection and abandonment
- Comparison, which leads to feeling either inferior or superior
- Busyness

Many of us have come to believe that admitting we have problems puts a blemish on our reputation.

It's painful to make yourself vulnerable with someone you thought was safe, only to be offered some pat, patronizing answer.

> Then the LORD God said, "It is not good for the man to be alone. I will make a helper who is just right for him."
> —Genesis 2:18

God created us for relationship; He wanted our love, freely given.

The first couple decided to exercise their ability to choose whether or not to obey the one and only restriction God had placed on them, and nothing has been the same ever since.

Adam and Eve brought upon themselves the curse of sin, which is physical and relational death.

In rare moments of intimacy, we get a glimpse of the kind of relationship God intended for us.

Bonding is that sense of intimate connectedness, of feeling safe and content in each other's presence; of truly knowing and truly being known.

An emotional wound may cause a person who once was open to go into hiding. And a person in hiding can't bond with anyone.

God wants us to be joined together, like the parts of a body.

> We are joined together in his body by his strong sinews, and we grow only as we get our nourishment and strength from God.
> —Colossians 2:19

> The human body has many parts, but the many parts make up only one body. So it is with the body of Christ.... Yes, the body has many different parts, not just one part. If the foot says, "I am not a part of the body because I am not a hand," that does not make it any less a part of the body. And if the ear says, "I am not part of the body because I am only an ear and not an eye," would that make it any less a part of the body? Suppose the whole body were an eye—then how would you hear? Or if your whole body were just one big ear, how could you smell anything? But God made our bodies with many parts, and he has put each part just where he wants it. What a strange thing a body would be if it had only one part! Yes, there are many parts, but only one body. The eye can never say to the hand, "I don't need you." The head can't say to the feet, "I don't need you."
> —1 Corinthians 12:12, 14–21

God created us for relationship, with Him and with one another, in spite of the risks involved—from exposure and rejection to arguments and bruised egos. It is only in community with Christ and His people that we receive the love, acceptance, emotional healing, safety, nurture, and comfort we need to be all Jesus intends us to be.

Talk It

1. Have you struggled at some point in your life (or perhaps your whole life) to establish satisfying friendships? If so, what are the explanations you have offered yourself to justify this struggle?

2. How has the fear of being known and possibly rejected played out in your life? Can you think of a situation in which you deliberately backed away from a friend just when she was beginning to see the real you?

3. Can you think of a time when you attempted to mislead others into thinking you had it together more than you really did?

4. Have you ever taken the risk of sharing some private emotion, wound, or struggle with someone you thought was safe, only to have your trust betrayed somehow? If so, how has this experience affected your ability to bond with others?

5. Colossians 2:19 says, "We are joined together in his body by his strong sinews, and we grow only as we get our nourishment and strength from God." What are your thoughts on the metaphor of the body of Christ, as expressed by Paul in this verse?

6. Are you ready to take the risk of trusting again? If not, what is holding you back?

Walk It

How can a person break both the walls and the vows that have built a fortress around her heart? Only by taking another risk. What relational risk will you take this week?

3

BEING THERE

Watch It

Eight Key Traits of Friendship:
- Affinity
- Availability
- Authenticity
- Ability to be at ease
- Affirmation
- Acceptance
- Accountability
- Assistance

Affinity

We shouldn't allow stereotypes and preconceived notions to limit our search for a friend.

Affinity has everything to do with passion—what makes you weep or pound your fists on the table or lie awake at night, too excited to sleep.

Finding a depth of commonality with another person usually requires some investigation. Discovering common passions can be as uncomplicated as learning to ask open-ended questions.

Finding affinity with someone is what makes diving into the friendship a pleasure rather than a duty.

> When others are happy, be happy with them. If they are sad, share their sorrow.
> —Romans 12:15

Availability

It is a terrible disappointment to be let down by a friend who promised to be there but wasn't—and an unexpected comfort to enjoy the presence of one who never said the words but just showed up.

You may have the most winsome personality in the world, but if you are not there for your friends when it counts, you lack the key trait of availability.

The people who need us the most often feel extremely reluctant to ask for help, to place themselves in a position of admitting a need, to impose on our busy schedules.

We are all needy at one time or another. In the company of a beloved friend, a smile becomes a celebration. A companion in life's valleys can keep us from the edge of despair. And the company of a friend on the mundane plateaus just makes life more interesting. The quality of availability is what enables us to infuse our friendships with all the other necessary traits.

Talk It

1. Have you ever befriended someone who initially did not seem "your type"? Describe your most prominent differences and then discuss why the friendship works anyway.

2. What are your primary passions in life, whether "shallow" (like shoe shopping) or profound (like stopping human trafficking)? Do you have friends who share those same passions?

3. Why and how do shared passions draw us to others?

4. Who has been there for you when it has counted?

5. Has there been a time when you looked for someone with whom to share a trial or a triumph, but no one was there to meet that need? Share or reflect on that experience. What were you really looking for in that moment?

6. How can we be tuned in enough to the needs of our closest friends so that we may be prepared to go to them when they lack the ability to ask for help?

7. Romans 12:15 says, "*When others are happy, be happy with them. If they are sad, share their sorrow.*" Try to think of some practical ways in which you could live out this verse in your relationships.

Walk It

How will you make yourself available to at least one friend this week? How will your communicate your availability to her?

4

THE BLONDE LEADING THE BLONDE

Watch It

Most of the time, the question "How are you?" elicits an insincere response—and it's often posed with equal insincerity.

The socially correct response to the query "How are you?" is "Fine." In most cases, the word *fine* is an acronym that means "feelings inside not expressed."

Authenticity

Here's an authentic question: "How is your heart?"

Pretending to be fine doesn't make our wounds go away; it only makes us feel lonelier.

Authenticity in a relationship must be both gradual and reciprocal.

If we never take the risk of beginning to trust someone, we will never know the satisfaction of a deeply authentic relationship.

Whether married or single, women thrive from sharing life's journey together.

There is very little satisfaction or comfort in a relationship between two people pretending to be people they aren't. That's called role-play, not relationship.

Oh! the blessing it is to have a friend to whom one can speak fearlessly on any subject; with whom one's deepest as well as one's most foolish thoughts come out simply and safely. Oh, the comfort—the inexpressible comfort of feeling safe with a person—having neither to weigh thoughts nor measure words, but pouring all right out, just as they are, chaff and grain together, certain that a faithful hand will take and sift them, keep what is worth keeping, and with the breath of kindness blow the rest away.[1]

Feeling at ease with someone is a quality of friendship that enables us to enjoy each other's presence, no matter our mood.

Affirmation

Most people on this planet are suffering from affirmation deprivation. Why is it that we are programmed to notice and name one another's shortcomings while downplaying or flat out disregarding their strengths?

The act of affirming someone means noticing her and validating who she is and what she does.

---

1. Dinah Mulock Craik, *A Life for a Life* (Leipzig: Bernhard Tauchnitz, 1859), 270.

"A person's words can be life-giving water" (Proverbs 18:4). We blossom like flowers nourished by fresh water and warm sunshine when someone expects the best of us and encourages us along the path in the pursuit of a goal, whether it's a big accomplishment or simply the survival of another day.

According to psychologists, it takes seven positive inputs to counteract one negative input.

Affirming a friend—noticing and naming her strengths and accomplishments—can refuel a weary soul, keeping her moving forward or even unleashing her potential.

Talk It

1. On a scale of 1 (not at all) to 10 (completely), how authentic are you with your friends regarding your thoughts and feelings?

2. Would you agree that even happily married women still need close female friends? Why or why not?

3. Recall a time when you took a risk and expressed difficult feelings with a friend who accepted and encouraged you. How did it change your relationship with that person?

4. Do you have a friend with whom you feel especially at ease? How do the two of you handle conflict in your relationship?

5. The Bible compares affirmation to physical necessities, such as food and water. Proverbs 18:20 says, *"Words satisfy the soul as food satisfies the stomach; the right words on a person's lips bring satisfaction."* Think of a time when a word of affirmation gave you the courage to reach for a challenging goal. Who affirmed you, what was said, and how did it affect you?

6. When was the last time you affirmed someone in your circle of friends? Whom can you affirm today?

Walk It

With whom do you need to have an authentic and/or affirming conversation this week? How will you make that happen?

5

A SOFT PLACE TO FALL

Watch It

Acceptance and Accountability

Acceptance and accountability work hand in hand. Acceptance says, "I love you just the way you are, so I won't try to change you, but I will support you in your efforts to change." Accountability says, "I love you too much to let you continue unchallenged in this way. I will courageously call out the best in you and be a truth teller in your life."

Jesus doesn't pressure me to become like Him in order for Him to accept me.

> We will speak the truth in love, growing in every way more and more like Christ, who is the head of his body, the church.
> —Ephesians 4:15 NLT07

Grace, as defined by Dr. Henry Cloud: "unbroken, uninterrupted, unearned, accepting relationship."

> How blessed is God! And what a blessing he is! He's the Father of our Master, Jesus Christ, and takes us to the high places of blessing in him. Long before he laid down earth's foundations, he had us in mind, had settled on us as the focus of his love, to be made whole and holy by his love. Long, long ago he decided to adopt us into his family through Jesus Christ. (What pleasure he took in planning this!) He wanted us to enter into the celebration of his lavish gift-giving by the hand of his beloved Son.
> —Ephesians 1:3–6 MSG

Isaiah 64:6 says, "We are all infected and impure with sin. When we proudly display our righteous deeds, we find they are but filthy rags." In this verse, the prophet wasn't referring to dishrags or even dust rags. He meant soiled menstrual rags.

Romans 5:8 says, "*But God showed his great love for us by sending Christ to die for us while we were still sinners.*" If the holy God of heaven could accept us "*while we were still sinners,*" shouldn't one sinner be able to do the same for a fellow sinner?

Through the pages of the Bible, we can follow the path Jesus forged from one broken, damaged human being to another.

> *While Jesus was having dinner at Matthew's house, many tax collectors and "sinners" came and ate with him and his disciples. When the Pharisees saw this, they asked his disciples, "Why does your teacher eat with tax collectors and 'sinners'?" On hearing this, Jesus said, "It is not the healthy who need a doctor, but the sick. But go and learn what this means: 'I desire mercy, not sacrifice.' For I have not come to call the righteous, but sinners."*
> —Matthew 9:10–13 NIV

John 8:32 says, "*You will know the truth, and the truth will set you free.*" Knowing the truth about ourselves frees us to grow into the people God wants us to be.

Proverbs 27:17 says, "As iron sharpens iron, a friend sharpens a friend." Being friends doesn't mean always agreeing with each other. If you love your friends, tell them the truth.

> If you love someone, you will be loyal to him no matter what the cost. You will always believe in him, always expect the best of him, and always stand your ground in defending him.
> —1 Corinthians 13:7 TLB

Assistance

Intimacy is key to offering assistance effectively. "Two people can accomplish more than twice as much as one; they get a better return for their labor. If one person falls, the other can reach out and help. But people who are alone when they fall are in real trouble" (Ecclesiastes 4:9–10).

Galatians 6:2 instructs us, "Carry each other's burdens, and in this way you will fulfill the law of Christ." To offer assistance to others, we ought to do for them what we would desire someone else do for us, were we in the same situation.

A friendship with acceptance and accountability is two people lovingly and courageously calling out the best in each other and being truth tellers in each other's lives.

Bearing another's burden means putting her needs above our own at times. To love and care for another as we love and care for ourselves. That's the law of Christ, and by sharing a friend's burden, we are fulfilling that law.

Talk It

1. When is it appropriate to hold someone accountable?

2. How does God's acceptance of us when we were sinners demonstrate the tension between grace and truth? (See Isaiah 64:6; Romans 5:8.)

3. How does God use friends to free each other? (See John 8:32; Proverbs 27:17; James 5:16.) Can you think of an example from your own experience?

4. Ecclesiastes 4:9–10 says, "*Two people can accomplish more than twice as much as one; they get a better return for their labor. If one person falls, the other can reach out and help. But people who are alone when they fall are in real trouble.*" Recall a time when you fell into trouble. Who was there to help you up? What did that person do that was particularly meaningful?

5. Which of the three traits of friendship we discussed in this chapter—acceptance, accountability, and assistance—do you most need today? Which is the hardest for you to offer to others? Why?

Walk It

How will you practice the trait you identified as most difficult for you in the coming week? How will you communicate to those closest to you that you are open to being held accountable for your words and deeds?

6

HOW TO BUILD A FRIENDSHIP

Watch It

There is something powerful about shared experiences—they tend to bind us together in unique, inextricable ways.

Shared histories provide a context for trust to be built; we learn, from the patterns of the past, that these people are going to be there for us.

A small group of close, committed friends can help one another become who they really want to be, even when they lack the strength or conviction to pursue those identities on their own.

David and Jonathan had a beautiful friendship.

> After David had finished talking with Saul, he met Jonathan, the king's son. There was an immediate bond of love between them, and they became the best of friends. From that day on, Saul kept David with him at the palace and wouldn't let him return home. And Jonathan made a special vow to be David's friend, and he sealed the pact by giving him his robe, tunic, sword, bow, and belt.
> —1 Samuel 18:1–4

> And Saul's son Jonathan went to David at Horesh and helped him find strength in God.
> —1 Samuel 16:23 NIV

Confidentiality

The more open we are with one another—the deeper our forays into each other's experiences—the more we strengthen our foundation of trust and deepen the intimacy of our friendship.

Intimacy cannot flourish without trust, and trust takes time to grow.

The Seasons of Friendship:
- Spring: a time of excitement and freshness
- Summer: a time when trust is built and you begin to experience intimacy
- Autumn: by now, you've heard her stories so many times, you could tell them yourself
- Winter: A woman who doesn't let her guard down, doesn't speak her heart, and doesn't listen to the heart of her friend will never experience the coziness of winter.

It is only as we invest our time, our energy, and our hearts in others, intertwining our stories with theirs over the years, that we build friendships tall and strong enough to shelter us from the harshness of life's storms.

Talk It

1. When have you had the experience of becoming friends with a group of people over a common experience?

2. Donna used the metaphor of a rowing team to illustrate how friends help one another. Can you remember a time when your "team" kept you moving forward when you lacked the strength yourself?

3. How can you help a friend to find her strength in God, as Jonathan did for David? (See 1 Samuel 23:16.)

4. How important is the principle of the red cloth in a group of friends? Can you recall a time when this principle has been violated by someone you trusted? Have you violated it yourself?

_____

_____

_____

5. How many of your friendships have made it through the seasons, all the way to the maturity of winter? Which season are most of your friendships in now? Can you identify anything specific that has prevented your friendships from reaching maturity?

_____

_____

_____

Walk It

I commit to pray this week about the awkward conversation I have been avoiding with _____.

7

TOXIC FRIENDSHIPS

Watch It

Remember these wise words: "Show me your friends, and I'll show you your future."

Proverbs 13:20 says, *"Whoever walks with the wise will become wise; whoever walks with fools will suffer harm."* A fool is unteachable and arrogant, and if she is a friend, her influence on us can only cause us pain.

The difference between a friendship infected with a temporary virus and one poisoned with a deadly toxin has to do with teachability.

Envy is simply wanting what belongs to someone else.

> Anger is cruel, and wrath is like a flood, but who can survive the destructiveness of jealousy ["envy" KJV]?
> —Proverbs 27:4

In His sovereignty and wisdom, God brings people into our lives who shine a spotlight on the places in our hearts that are wounded, calloused, or bruised.

When we can truly accept, love, and forgive ourselves, then we can do the same for others, even when their flaws are painfully familiar.

Gossip is the sharing of information about other people, true or not, that causes others to think less highly of them.

> A gossip tells secrets, so don't hang around with someone who talks too much.
> —Proverbs 20:19

> Do not spread slanderous gossip
> among your people.
> —Leviticus 19:16

Gossip has just as much to do with what's going on inside of us as it does with what's observed and overheard by the people around us.

One way or another, what's inside comes out.

> A good person produces good deeds from a good heart, and an evil person produces evil deeds from an evil heart. Whatever is in your heart determines what you say.
> —Luke 6:45

I want to have a friend, and I want to be a friend, who is so filled with good stuff on the inside that when pressure is applied, what spills out is good, with a fragrance that blesses everyone in the room.

> The heartfelt counsel of a friend is as sweet as perfume.
> —Proverbs 27:9

What do you do when a friend wants to spill gossip?

- Make it about you, not about her.
- Answer every negative statement about the verbal victim with a positive one.

Discontentment is a trait of someone who is always unhappy about something and easily finds fault with just about anything.

What we focus our attention on, good or bad, begins to take over our lives and then spreads, affecting (or infecting) the lives of others.

Contentment doesn't come automatically, even when we get what we want.

> *I have learned to be content whatever the circumstances. I know what it is to be in need, and I know what it is to have plenty. I have learned the secret of being content in any and every situation, whether well fed or hungry, whether living in plenty or in want. I can do everything through him who gives me strength.*
> —Philippians 4:11–13 NIV

Narcissism is an exceptional interest in or admiration for oneself.

Some people go through life believing that everyone else exists to meet their needs, help them accomplish their goals, and make them happy.

Usually it is an avalanche of small, disrespectful acts that kills a friendship over time.

As soon as you establish healthy, nonnegotiable boundaries, a narcissist will likely walk away.

The only way a narcissist will grow up to experience loving relationships is if her selfish patterns of behavior no longer succeed in getting her what she wants.

Toxicity Diagnostic Question #1: Is my friend directionally challenged?

"People are not morally neutral. They either influence our lives for good or for evil. They help us become what they are."[2]

Toxicity Diagnostic Test #2: Is my friend teachable?

When our friend is confronted with the truth about her toxic behavior, will she listen?

> Do your part to live in peace with everyone, as much as possible.
> —Romans 12:18

Pray for our friend and ourselves.

Explain our position.

Act out of love.

Continue to be kind.

Enlist the help of Christian friends.

—Jean Shaw

---

2. Gary Inrig, *Quality Friendship: The Risks and Rewards* (Chicago: Moody Press, 1981), 126.

We can remove someone from our intimate circle without kicking her out of our lives entirely.

We should use the lessons learned from the pain of a toxic friendship to make us wise, and we ought to address any issues in our hearts that the conflict may have brought to light.

Talk It

1. In what ways have you seen envy affect friendship?

2. Have you ever experienced a friend's behavior shining a spotlight on something about yourself that you disliked? How did you respond to that discomfort?

3. Do you struggle with gossip—internal, external, or both? If so, brainstorm some ways of rerouting your thoughts and/or conversations.

4. What do you believe is the secret of contentment? (See Philippians 4:11–13.)

5. Gary Inrig wrote, "People are not morally neutral. They either influence our lives for good or for evil. They help us become what they are." Do you agree? What are your thoughts on your circle of friends in light of that statement?

6. Romans 12:18 says, *"Do your part to live in peace with everyone, as much as possible."* Thinking of the people in your life, have you done your part?

Walk It

How will you intentionally be a healthy friend? What steps will you take to limit the influence of toxic people in your life?

8

MENDING FENCES

Watch It

Relationship reality check: people get hurt.

The goal of restoration is to recreate the friendship, making it better than it was before.

The Bible gives us clear instructions for handling discord in relationships:

Take the Initiative

Whether we hurt someone else or someone else has hurt us, the ball is always in our court.

> If you enter your place of worship and, about to make an offering, you suddenly remember a grudge a friend has against you, abandon your offering, leave immediately, go to this friend and make things right. Then and only then, come back and work things out with God. Or say you're out in the street and an old enemy accosts you. Don't lose a minute. Make the first move; make things right with him.
> —Matthew 5:23–25 MSG

> If a fellow believer hurts you, go and tell him—work it out between the two of you. If he listens, you've made a friend.
> —Matthew 18:15 MSG

We are not to be prickly people.

> People with good sense restrain their anger; they earn esteem by overlooking wrongs.
> —Proverbs 19:11

> Be humble and gentle. Be patient with each other, making allowance for each other's faults because of your love. Try always to be led along together by the Holy Spirit and so be at peace with one another.
> —Ephesians 4:2–3 TLB

> Make every effort to live in peace with all men....
> —Hebrews 12:14 NIV

> Most important of all, continue to show deep love for each other, for love covers a multitude of sins.
> —1 Peter 4:8

"Make every effort...." "Most important of all...." The Word of God is pretty serious about relational unity.

The goal of a confrontation is not to win a battle; it is to win back a friend.

> If another believer sins against you, go privately and point out the fault. If the other person listens and confesses it, you have won that person back. But if you are unsuccessful, take one or two others with you and go back again, so that everything you say may be confirmed by two or three witnesses.
> —Matthew 18:15–16

First we should humble ourselves and ask God to reveal the condition of our own hearts before we approach someone else about the condition of hers. Second, we must conduct ourselves with gentleness, as tenderly as a mother would extract a sliver of wood from the eye of her child.

> Stop judging others, and you will not be judged. For others will treat you as you treat them. Whatever measure you use in judging others, it will be used to measure how you are judged. And why worry about a speck in your friend's eye when you have a log in your own? How can you think of saying, "Let me help you get rid of that speck in your eye," when you can't see past the log in your own eye? Hypocrite! First get rid of the log from your own eye; then perhaps you will see well enough to deal with the speck in your friend's eye.
> —Matthew 7:1–5

A person with moral authority is one who is widely respected because of a track record of quality character, behavior, and decision making.

Keeping peace often means shoveling unhealed wounds and unkind words under the carpet; *making peace* sometimes involves confrontation, but the confrontation always entails forgiveness.

Time alone won't heal a broken heart!

What about justice?

> It was our weaknesses he carried; it was our sorrows that weighed him down....He was wounded and crushed for our sins. He was beaten that we might have peace. He was whipped, and we were healed! All of us have strayed away like sheep. We have left God's paths to follow our own. Yet the Lord laid on him the guilt and sins of us all.
> —Isaiah 53:4–6

Forgiveness engages the will.

- First, we must make a decision to forgive
- Second, we decide to walk the path of forgiveness

It's important to surrender your

> Since God chose you to be the holy people whom he loves, you must clothe yourselves with tender-hearted mercy, kindness, humility, gentleness, and patience. You must make allowance for each other's faults and forgive the person who offends you. Remember, the Lord forgave you, so you must forgive others. And the most important piece of clothing you must wear is love. Love is what binds us all together in perfect harmony.
> —Colossians 3:12–14

expectations, because they are the cause of virtually all conflict and stress in life.

It's okay to make our needs and wants clear, but we have no right to demand that our friends meet our expectations.

Expectation is different from expectancy.

> Where do you think all these appalling wars and quarrels come from? Do you think they just happen? Think again. They come about because you want your own way, and fight for it deep inside yourselves. You lust for what you don't have and are willing to kill to get it. You want what isn't yours and will risk violence to get your hands on it.
> —James 4:1–2 MSG

We can't manage our relationships our own way, with no regard for God, and expect Him to bless them. He formed our hearts, and He knows how they work. But we can honor God and invite His presence and blessing into our friendships as we take the initiative to be peacemakers and as we confront lovingly, forgive liberally, and surrender our expectations to Him.

Talk It

1. Think of a time when a friend wounded you in some way. Did you confront your friend? Did you just allow the friendship to slip away? How do you feel about that decision now?

2. Why is it so important that we pray for discernment before we confront someone? Matthew 7:3–5 provides one reason, but there are more.

3. Have you ever approached conflict resolution using the steps laid out in Matthew 18:15–17? If so, what was the result? If not, why do you think you were reluctant to follow these steps?

4. Again, Dr. Larry Crabb said this: "Certainly we struggle as victims of other people's unkindness. We have been sinned against. But we cannot excuse our sinful responses to others on the grounds of their mistreatment of us. We are responsible for what we do. We are both strugglers and sinners, victims and agents, people who hurt and people who harm." What are some evidences from your own experience of the truth of these statements?

5. How is it possible for justice to be served if the person who offended us never pays for what was done? (See Isaiah 53:4–6.)

6. In what ways might your friendships improve if you started employing God's guidelines for relationship management?

Walk It

Fill in the blanks below after prayerfully considering how to do so.

I will confront _____ about _____.

I will forgive _____ for _____.

I will ask forgiveness of _____ for _____.

9

WHEN YOU CAN'T FIND A FRIEND

Watch It

Take a close look...

- inward, to evaluate whether we are quality friendship material.
- outward, to see who is available for friendship right now.
- upward, to ask God to bring someone new into our lives and/or to open our eyes.

You need to know who you are and what you have to offer in a relationship.

To God, human beings are priceless.

If the whole world decided you were worthless, it would not change your essential value. Why? Because as a believer you share both the image and nature of the unchanging God Himself. Your value is tied to Him. He is the magnetic north pole of your essential worth. The Almighty Creator is the infinite reference point, the ultimate standard, the "cosmic blue book" of your value. He made you in His image and likeness. Your value was written in blood at the cross. And whatever He values is valuable.[3]

Making friends usually requires action. Seldom does God providentially drop a new companion in our lap.

Your heavenly Father knows your needs. He may have a purpose in isolating you for a period of time. And don't forget that He is always with you! He has given you this promise: *"Never will I leave you; never will I forsake you"* (Hebrews 13:5 NIV).

---

3. Joseph C. Aldrich, *Self-worth: How to Become More Loveable* (Portland: Multnomah Press, 1982).

We become malnourished and stunted when we connect to a different branch and try to get from it what the true Vine alone can provide.

> I am the true vine....Remain in me, and I will remain in you. For a branch cannot produce fruit if it is severed from the vine, and you cannot be fruitful apart from me. Yes, I am the vine; you are the branches. Those who remain in me, and I in them, will produce much fruit. For apart from me you can do nothing. Anyone who parts from me is thrown away like a useless branch and withers. Such branches are gathered into a pile to be burned. But if you stay joined to me and my words remain in you, you may ask any request you like, and it will be granted! My true disciples produce much fruit. This brings great glory to my Father.
> —John 15:1, 4–8

Isolation opens our spiritual eyes to recognize God's presence.

Invest in an ever-deepening friendship with God by spending time with Him daily. Ask Him to show you how to build health and intimacy into your primary relationships. Then, look for a friend with whom you can share the adventure.

Talk It

1. Reflecting on the relationships you have had throughout life, can you identify any tendencies in yourself that have been detrimental to establishing and/or maintaining friendships?

2. Do you ever struggle with self-worth? Why? What qualities do you possess that could enrich another person in a relationship? Be generous with yourself and name them.

3. Brainstorm some ways in which you might find a new friend and also how you could invite her into a friendship once you have found her.

4. We discussed a passage from John 15 in which Jesus compared His relationship with us to that of a vine and its branches. Which other branch(es) have you tried attaching yourself to instead of the true Vine? What have been the consequences of that attachment?

5. Think back to a period of loneliness or friendlessness in your life. Might God have had a lesson for you to learn through that time? If so, what was it?

6. Do you consider God to be a Friend? If not, what would it take for you to invite Him into your life?

Walk It

Choose to believe what God says about your worth. Make a list to remind yourself of what you have to offer others in friendship.

_____

_____

_____

_____

_____

10

THE PERFECT FRIEND

Watch It

God's great heart yearns for our friendship.

We have the power to grievously wound the heart of almighty God. We can reject Him. The choice is ours.

> Though he was God, he did not demand and cling to his rights as God. He made himself nothing; he took the humble position of a slave and appeared in human form. And in human form he obediently humbled himself even further by dying a criminal's death on a cross.
> —Philippians 2:6–8

In God's sovereignty and wisdom, the danger, the dark side of Christmas, became Good Friday. Somehow Jesus, the only sinless Man, hung condemned of every rape, child molestation, murder, theft, and lie.

> Greater love has no one than this, that he lay down his life for his friends.
> —John 15:13 NIV

> This is how we know what love is: Jesus Christ laid down his life for us.
> —1 John 3:16 NIV

No one but Jesus can offer you perfect friendship.

> My purpose is to give life in all its fullness.
> —John 10:10

If you know Jesus personally, you are never without hope.

Entering into friendship with Jesus requires a sincere heart and a simple expression of a few words that are necessary in every friendship: *sorry, thank you,* and *please.*

Sorry: We must express to Him our awareness that we have wronged Him by living independently of Him and making selfish choices.

Thank You: We need to acknowledge His incredible sacrifice in sending His Son to satisfy the demands of justice for our wrongs.

Please: We surrender control, asking Him to take over the leadership of our lives.

As in any friendship, we can go deeper with God only by spending time with Him.

What an amazing privilege it is to be able to meet with God, anytime, anywhere! He is always ready and willing to commune with us. Talk to Him. Listen to Him. Worship Him. Then, pray with me: Praise to You, dear Jesus, King of Kings and Lord of Lords! You are above all, sovereign and omnipotent. Thank You for choosing to use Your power to become powerless. Thank You for the wisdom and love that drove You to become a sovereign victim so that I could become Your friend.

Talk It

1. Did anything about Donna's description of God's radical rescue mission make you think differently about Jesus' love for you? Explore those thoughts.

2. How does walking through life in relationship with God change the quality of a person's life? (See John 10:10.) If you have invited Jesus into your life, how has His friendship changed things for you?

3. Most believers feel disappointed with God at some point in their lives. This sense of disillusionment is not caused by God's failure but by our faulty perspective. How might our periods of disappointment be different if we were to take the approach of the apostle Peter in John 6:66–69?

4. We discussed the importance of saying "Sorry," "Thank You," and "Please" to God. If you have never invited Jesus to be your Friend, why not make today the day you express to Him those words that are necessary in all friendships?

5. How can you begin growing in intimacy with God?

Walk It

Write out your heart's desire for your relationship with God.

CONCLUSION

Watch It

Darlene to God: "You created me for this, and You gave me these desires. Why aren't You fulfilling them?

God to Brian: "You haven't begun to imagine how good life can be yet. Trust Me."

God to Darlene: "My child, this is who you have been waiting for. Let Brian be an expression of My love for you. Trust Me."

I believe strongly and with more conviction than any other point in my life that the God I love, the God that loves me, is a sovereign God, He is a good God, and His love and grace are available to us in the good times and in the hard times. Would I have chosen for the man I love, his wife, Sonja, and their children to walk through a twelve-year journey of suffering? No. Would I have chosen to be alone for twenty-plus years? No. Do I now understand some of the whys I asked over the years? Yes. I believe that when God fashioned me in my mother's womb, He created me for Brian and the boys, for this period in their lives."

—Darlene

Talk It

1. Darlene spoke of struggling with God over the "whys" of life as they related to her desire to have a family of her own. "You created me for this, and You gave me these desires. Why aren't You fulfilling them?" Can you relate to that kind of struggle? What are some of the "whys" of your life?

2. Donna wrote, "I have had a front-row seat watching this new family come together, and God's hand in it has been unmistakable." In what ways has God's hand been present in weaving together the circumstances in your life? Is it possible you have attributed to luck or coincidence what was, in reality, God's active participation in your life?

3. If your life was suddenly taken from you, who loves you deeply enough to keep your memory alive?

4. Do you share a deepening friendship with God?

Walk It

What spiritual practices will you adopt in order to cultivate your friendship with God?

_____

_____

_____

_____

_____

READ BEFORE YOU LEAD

Thank you for your willingness to facilitate the important conversations that take place after the teaching DVDs in this series. The love you express to the women in your group is far more important than your ability to say the right thing every time. Please read through the suggestions below for all the weeks *before* your first session. That way, you will know what is coming and have time to pray, prepare, and share. I will be praying for you, that you will seek and hear the Holy Spirit as you shepherd this little flock God has entrusted to you.

—*Donna*

Chapter One
Just One Friend

The first time a group of women meet, they are naturally guarded. They are seeking affinity and testing trust. In this first session, it's okay to keep the conversation light, even to let it remain at the surface level. Encourage the women to share, as they feel comfortable, from their own experiences with friendship and to comment on the questions and content of the session, but be sure to let the conversation to flow naturally.

Don't panic if sharing is stilted and punctuated with silences, because silence often means people are sifting through their own memories and thinking about how the question applies to them. The discussion will become more profound and lively as the women begin to feel at ease with one another. The goal of today is to begin to lay the foundation of that affinity and trust.

If the subject comes up, and you have time, you could talk about the story of Jonathan and David. To prepare for this possibility, read 1 Samuel chapters 16–20, with a particular focus on chapter 20, verses 14–17 and 41–42.

Chapter Two
Everyone Needs a Friend

This week, you will begin to explore the reasons we tend to hide behind self-constructed walls and masks. This is a good time to talk about confidentiality, reminding the women that whatever is shared around the table must remain at the table. You might even ask those who are willing to agree to this covenant of confidentiality to express that out loud. (I would avoid going around the table and putting people "on the spot" in doing this.) But if the majority voluntarily declares they will keep the group's confidences, the door may be opened to the genuine sharing of hearts.

Questions may come up this week about the fall of mankind into sin and the curse of sin. Here are some Scriptures you may want to consult in order to clarify these topics for the participants: Genesis 2:15; 3; Romans 3:23–27; 8:1–16.

Remember, it's okay if you don't know all the answers. If a question comes up that stumps you, admit it and then offer to do some research. Your coach, pastor, or leader will be able to help you with this. You can also consult helpful Web sites, such as biblegateway.com and blueletterbible.org.

Chapter Three
Being There

This week, I want to remind you that silences are likely more awkward for you as the facilitator than they are for the group members. Resist the urge to fill up every lull in conversation with your own stories or to quickly move on to the next question. Instead, allow the women time to think about how each question applies to them. Having said that, week three is a good time to begin asking specific people to respond, by saying, for example, "What do you think about that, Jen?" Some of the more introverted group members may not share unless invited to do so. Ask the Holy Spirit to make you sensitive to what is going on inside each group member's heart.

Chapter Four
The Blonde Leading the Blonde

If you haven't been praying together at your group sessions, this would be a good time to start. Remind the participants about the sacred trust of confidentiality. Be sure to leave time at the end of your session to allow the sharing of *personal* prayer requests. (This is not the time to pray for your neighbor's aunt's dog's injured paw.) You can pray together, if time permits, or assign each request to a volunteer within the group who then agrees to pray daily over the next week for that need.

Chapter Five
A Soft Place to Fall

For this week's session, the participants will need their Bibles. Bring a few extra, if you're able, for those who may have forgotten theirs or who may not own one. If the group members are new to the faith, or if you aren't sure where they are on their spiritual journeys, be sure to use a more modern version that is easier to understand, such as the *New Living Translation*, the *Amplified Bible*, or *The Message*. It is good to use a variety of translations and paraphrases to squeeze out the full meaning of a passage. Try to source inexpensive modern translations from your church or ministry that can be given away or sold inexpensively to group members who don't own a modern translation of the Bible.

Chapter Six
How to Build a Friendship

You might consider bring a red square of fabric (a red cloth napkin works well) to your meeting from this week until the end of the study. Unfold it at the beginning of the conversation time, reminding the women in your group what it means. Then, make a point of folding it up after your prayer time, symbolizing the safekeeping of all that has been shared within the group.

Chapter Seven
Toxic Friendships

You are likely nearing a point in this study when the women feel at ease with each other enough to share freely. You may find that you don't have time to "get through" all the suggested discussion questions. That's okay. The point of the questions is to facilitate reflection and conversation and to help you focus your sharing on the topic of the day. Feel free to skip over any questions that you think are less relevant to the women in your group. You may need to ask a quieter individual what she thinks about a question in order to make space for her to share. Try to give each participant opportunity rather than allowing one or two people to dominate the discussions. As you get to know them and rely on the Holy Spirit for guidance, you will know where to steer the conversation so that it is most beneficial for your little flock.

Chapter Eight
Mending Fences

In this session, you are entering really tender territory. Come prepared to share deeply from your own experiences—and not just the ones with happy endings. Allow others to share first, but lead the way with your own stories if your group members seem reluctant to go to such deep places of the heart. Suggest the idea of holding each other accountable to take the steps the Holy Spirit may be directing individuals to take, such as confronting and forgiving.

Chapter Nine
When You Can't Find a Friend

This could be a difficult session for someone who struggles in social settings and relationships. If one or more women in your group has expressed this struggle, or if you know that someone has low self-esteem, practice honest affirmation today when you get to question 2. Invite the group members to name the positive qualities they have seen in each other. If you perceive any negative or toxic tendencies in a member, pray about asking her privately, outside of the session, if she feels it would be helpful to her to hear what you see as the reason(s) she may be unsuccessful in friendships. The goal of this session—and of what takes place before and after it—is to help each other grow in the ability to find great friends as well as to be great friends.

Chapter Ten
The Perfect Friend

This session could be the most important day of someone's entire life—her *eternal* life. Bathe this session in prayer, asking the Holy Spirit to open the spiritual eyes and hearts of women in your group who have never invited Jesus to be their Friend. When you get to question 4, ask if there is anyone in your group who is at a point of wanting to invite Jesus into relationship with her. For those who say yes, be prepared to lead them in a time of prayer, with everyone around your table bowing in honor of the sacredness of this moment. I suggest not using a "repeat after me" prayer but rather asking the members to use the three words *sorry, thank you,* and *please* as an outline for their own personal, silent prayers. When they have finished praying, invite the others to give thanks to God for expanding His family in the moments you have shared together. Celebrate your new relationship as sisters in Christ before you continue with your conversation around the remaining questions.

Conclusion

Today we close the loop of my friendship journey with Sonja. In your conversation time, encourage your group members to discern the ways in which God, in His grace, uses even our suffering for our ultimate good. When your discussion time is over, pray together. Then, decide how you want the friendships that have deepened within your group to continue. You might choose to continue meeting to discuss another book, or you might just have a party to celebrate how you've grown in relationship with God and with each other!

ABOUT THE AUTHOR

Donna Carter has a unique ability to synthesize life experience into digestible life lessons. She is sought as a speaker across the globe because of her clarity and humor, as well as the lightbulb moments she triggers for people seeking help on their spiritual journeys.

Her first book, *10 Smart Things Women Can Do to Build a Better Life*, was released in the fall of 2007 and is now being distributed in five countries. The DVD life management course by the same name is an outreach tool that is working its way around the world, making appearances in Islamic countries, developing nations, and communist countries, as well as U.S. military bases.

Donna has traveled widely and is passionate about social justice, especially helping women and children achieve their full potential. Her recent adventures include connecting with the underground church in China, experiencing the catastrophic earthquake in Haiti, and linking Canadian women with young mothers living in abject poverty in El Salvador through Compassion International.

Donna and her husband, Randy, are the cofounders of Straight Talk Ministries, a nonprofit organization committed to helping people find faith and apply it to everyday life. They live in Calgary, a thriving city in the shadow of the Canadian Rockies.

Donna and Randy have two young adult daughters and a newly acquired son-in-law.

Formerly an interior designer by profession, Donna has decided to devote the rest of her career life to helping people live purposefully through her speaking and writing.

Donna may be contacted for speaking engagements at www.donnacarter.org.

⌒

A portion of the proceeds of this book have been designated to Compassion's Child Survival Program–ES 21 in El Salvador. To join Donna in reaching out to children in the developing world through Compassion International, visit www.compassion.com (for residents of the United States) or compassion.ca (for residents of Canada).